The Secret Life of
Trees

FIRST EDITION
Project Editor Naia Bray-Moffatt; **Art Editor** Jane Horne; **Senior Editor** Mary Atkinson;
Managing Art Editor Peter Bailey; **US Editor** Regina Kahney; **Pre-Production Producer** Nadine King;
Producer Sara Hu; **Picture Researcher** Liz Moore; **Natural History Consultant** Theresa Greenaway;
Reading Consultant Linda Gambrell, PhD

THIS EDITION
Editorial Management by Oriel Square
Produced for DK by WonderLab Group LLC
Jennifer Emmett, Erica Green, Kate Hale, *Founders*

Editors Grace Hill Smith, Libby Romero, Maya Myers, Michaela Weglinski;
Photography Editors Kelley Miller, Annette Kiesow, Nicole DiMella; **Managing Editor** Rachel Houghton;
Designers Project Design Company; **Researcher** Michelle Harris; **Copy Editor** Lori Merritt;
Indexer Connie Binder; **Proofreader** Larry Shea; **Reading Specialist** Dr. Jennifer Albro;
Curriculum Specialist Elaine Larson

Published in the United States by DK Publishing
1745 Broadway, 20th Floor, New York, NY 10019

Copyright © 2023 Dorling Kindersley Limited
DK, a Division of Penguin Random House LLC
23 24 25 26 10 9 8 7 6 5 4 3 2 1
001-333899-June/2023

All rights reserved.

Without limiting the rights under the copyright reserved above, no part of this publication may be reproduced, stored in or introduced into a retrieval system, or transmitted, in any form, or by any means (electronic, mechanical, photocopying, recording, or otherwise), without the prior written permission of the copyright owner.
Published in Great Britain by Dorling Kindersley Limited

A catalog record for this book
is available from the Library of Congress.
HC ISBN: 978-0-7440-7196-2
PB ISBN: 978-0-7440-7197-9

DK books are available at special discounts when purchased in bulk for sales promotions, premiums,
fundraising, or educational use. For details, contact: DK Publishing Special Markets,
1745 Broadway, 20th Floor, New York, NY 10019
SpecialSales@dk.com

Printed and bound in China

The publisher would like to thank the following for their kind permission to reproduce their images:
a=above; c=center; b=below; l=left; r=right; t=top; b/g=background
123RF.com: filmfoto 23tr, Svetlana Yefimkina 31bc; **Alamy Stock Photo:** Jonathan Mbu (Pura Vida Exotics) 27bl;
Dreamstime.com: Dink101 10-11t, Juhku 16, Ivan Kmit 14-15b, Stanislav Komogorov 28t, Stephen Moehle 7cr, Osipovfoto 12br,
Sally Scott 25t, Heather Snow 10bl, Sandra Standbridge 17br, Tom Wang 29tr; **Getty Images:** Raphael Schneider 19b
Cover images: *Front:* **Dreamstime.com:** Leerobin l, Webpainterstd; *Back:* **Shutterstock.com:** kstudija cra;
Spine: **Dreamstime.com:** Leerobin b, Webpainterstd

All other images © Dorling Kindersley
For more information see: www.dkimages.com

For the curious
www.dk.com

Level 2

The Secret Life of Trees

Chiara Chevallier

Contents

6 The Parts of a Tree
14 Broad-Leaved Trees
22 Conifers
26 It Comes From a Tree!

30 Glossary
31 Index
32 Quiz

The Parts of a Tree

Trees are all around us.
But what do you really know about them?
What secrets do they hold?
When you look at a tree, what do you see?

You see bark that protects the tree's trunk and branches.
The bark at the bottom of the tree is old.
It is rough and cracked.
At the top, the bark is young and smooth.

bark

Towering Heights

The tallest tree alive today is over 380 feet (116 m) high! It is a coast redwood growing in California. The tree is called Hyperion, after a Titan in Greek mythology. Its name means "The High One."

When you look at a tree, you can only see half of it! The other half is underground. These are the roots, pushing their way through the thick earth.

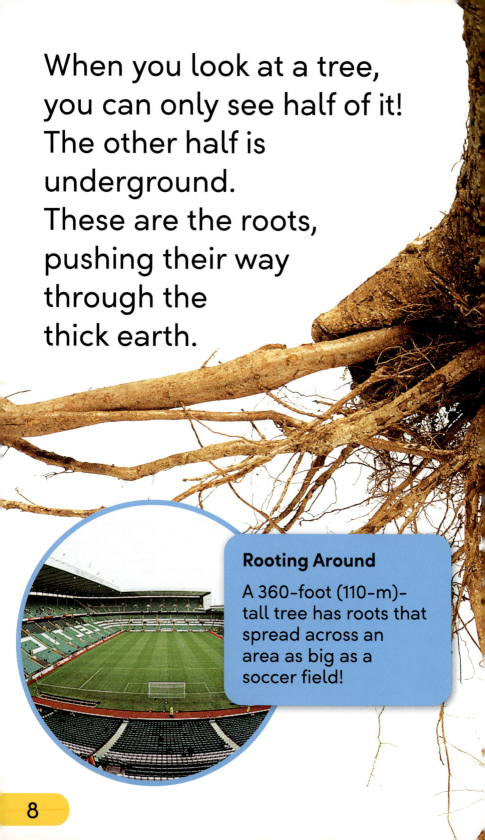

Rooting Around

A 360-foot (110-m)-tall tree has roots that spread across an area as big as a soccer field!

Roots can be as long as the height of the tree.

A tree can live longer than all other living things. It can live for hundreds— even thousands—of years!

Ancient Pine

The oldest recorded tree in the world is a bristlecone pine. It is over 5,000 years old.

A tree needs sunlight and water to grow.

High above the ground, the tree's leaves use energy from the Sun to make food. Below the ground, the tree's roots spread out in search of water.

A tree is a home for many animals.

High up in the branches, birds carefully build nests. They lay their eggs out of sight and out of reach of other animals.

Under the tree branches, wasps may build a nest.

Insects and bugs live on and under a tree's bark.

Insect Disguise

Some insects, like these thorn bugs, disguise themselves as part of a tree so they don't get eaten.

In the ground, under the roots of a tree, rabbits and badgers dig their homes.

A tree in the summer is an animal hotel!

Broad-Leaved Trees

Trees come in all shapes and sizes, but there are two main types of trees:

A broad-leaved tree has large, flat leaves on its wide-spreading branches. The shady green forests of eastern North America are mostly made up of broad-leaved trees.

Many broad-leaved trees change their leaves as the seasons change.

As the chill of winter sets in, most broad-leaved trees lose their leaves.
The leaves drop off because there is less sunlight.

As spring begins, fresh new leaves open from buds on the branches.
The tree wakes up from its winter sleep as the days get longer and there is more sunlight.

By summer, the tree is covered with bright, green leaves. The leaves give shade, shelter, and food to many animals and insects.

As the weather gets colder in the misty autumn, the tree's leaves change color.
Some leaves turn brown.
Others turn bright yellow or brilliant red.
Then, they fall to the ground.
The tree is getting ready to sleep again until next spring.

New trees can start to grow when older trees drop their seeds on the ground.

Growing Acorns

In one summer, a fully grown oak tree can produce up to 50,000 acorns!

A seed faces many dangers.
Hungry animals may eat it.
It may be stepped on
and crushed.
Most seeds never survive to
grow into a tree.

Broad-leaved
trees protect
their seeds.
Some put them
in a hard shell,
like an acorn
or a chestnut.

Conifers

Not all trees lose their leaves in winter. Some, like conifers, are evergreens.

Conifers can live in colder places than most broad-leaved trees can. Instead of wide, flat leaves, they have short, sharp needles.

needles

Bouncy Branches

The branches of a conifer are extra bouncy. This keeps them from snapping, even when covered with thick snow.

Conifer trees produce hard, scaly cones to protect their seeds.

Cones come in different sizes. Some are less than half an inch (1 cm) long. The cone of the sugar pine is 2 feet (60 cm) long.

A pine cone can help you forecast the weather!
When it is warm, the scales of the cone open up.
They close again when a storm is on the way.
This keeps the seeds dry.

It Comes From a Tree!

Wherever you are in the world, you can usually find trees. Tropical trees grow in the warmest places.
Lots of tasty fruits and nuts—such as avocados, dates, mangoes, and Brazil nuts—come from tropical trees.

Coconut palms grow wild on many tropical beaches. This palm tree's seed is located inside its hairy coconut shell. The shell contains milk, so the seed can start growing—even if it is washed up somewhere dry.

Tree Houses

In tropical forests in Africa, chimpanzees spend nearly all their lives up in the trees. They only go down to the jungle floor to look for food.

Lots of other things come from trees, too.
When you look at a tree, you can see the source of wood and paper.

The table you sit at and the chair you sit on may be made of wood from trees.

The swing you play on may be made from wood.

And the biggest secret of all? Even the book you are reading comes from a tree!

Glossary

Bark
The tough outer covering of a woody root or stem

Branches
A part that grows out from a plant trunk or stem. Branches are also called limbs.

Bud
A small growth on a plant stem that develops into leaves or a flower

Broad-leaved tree
A tree with large, flat leaves that grow on wide-spreading branches

Conifer
A tree with short, sharp needles. A conifer is also called an evergreen.

Cone
The fruit of a conifer tree. It is covered with scales, which open to release the seeds.

Leaves
Flat parts, which are usually green, that grow from the branches or stem of a plant

Needles
The short, sharp leaves of a conifer tree

Roots
The part of a plant or tree that grows underground

Tropical
The warm, moist region near Earth's equator

Trunk
The main stem of a tree

Index

acorns 20, 21
animals 12–13, 18, 21, 27
bark 6, 7
birds 12
branches 6, 15, 23
bristlecone pine 10
broad-leaved trees 14–21
buds 17
chestnut 21
chimpanzees 27
coast redwood 7

coconut palm 27
color of leaves 15, 19
cones 24–25
conifers 14, 22–25
evergreens 22
forests 15
fruits 26
insects 12, 13, 18
leaves 11, 14–22
needles 22
nests 12
nuts 26
oak tree 20

pine cones 24–25
roots 8–9, 11
seasons 15–19
seeds 20–21, 24–25, 27
sugar pine 24
sunlight 11, 17
thorn bugs 13
tropical trees 26–27
trunk 6
wasps 12
water 11
wood 28, 29

31

Quiz

Answer the questions to see what you have learned. Check your answers in the key below.

1. Which part of a tree grows underground?
2. Which part of a tree uses energy from the Sun to make food?
3. What are the two types of trees?
4. Which type of tree produces hard, scaly cones?
5. Where is a coconut palm tree's seed located?

1. The roots 2. The leaves 3. Broad-leaved and conifer
4. A conifer 5. Inside its hairy coconut shell